Deali~~n~~

with thorns

An Evangelical Approach to Divorce, the Role of Women in Church and Human Sexuality in the Bible.

Peter M Phillips,
New Testament Tutor,
Cliff College

CLIFF COLLEGE PUBLISHING

CALVER, SHEFFIELD S30 1XG Tel: BASLOW (01246) 582321

ISBN 1 898362 16 5
© Cliff College Publishing

Cliff College Publishing,
Calver, Sheffield S30 1XG

Printed by

MOORLEY'S Print & Publishing
23 Park Rd., Ilkeston, Derbys DE7 5DA
Tel/Fax: (0115) 932 0643

from data supplied on disk

Some time ago, I was approached to offer some reflection on a very specific question that I have incorporated into the title of this book. As I attempted to do this, however, I felt that I must also raise the whole question of how we look at the Bible. In this book, I will look firstly at this question. I will then use the methodology proposed to look at the three areas outlined in the title.

Contents

Chapter 1
Methodology

As the phenomenon called 'postmodernism' has developed over the last few years, society's foundational myths have been renamed 'metanarratives'. A 'metanarrative' represents those truths which dictated the way in which society has formed itself - truths which have regulated this formation as well. Steven Connor talks of metanarratives as "those guiding principles and mythologies which once seemed to control, delimit and interpret all the diverse forms of discursive activity in the world"[1]. In the field of literary criticism this means that a 'metanarrative' is the theological, sociological and philosophical background to any particular narrative.

Some would argue that the whole postmodernist debate has attempted to abolish, or at least called into question these metanarratives. This view is seen in Jean-François Lyotard's insistence that postmodernism is summed up in the "suspicion of metanarratives", in "the dissolution of every kind of totalizing narrative which claims to govern the whole field of social activity and representation"[2]. Postmodernism, however, is notoriously difficult to pin down. Lyotard's doctrine of suspicion becomes one more cliché used by those who seek to define this indefinable whirlwind of philosophical and cultural confusion[3]. As with most clichés, there is both understanding and misunderstanding here. Postmodernism seeks to break down all absolute statements. It is absolutes that it is seeking to destroy - not the metanarratives; much of postmodernism is simply a change from one metanarrative to another[4]. Indeed, some forms of postmodern literary theory argue strongly for 'metanarrative'.

---

[1] Steven Connor, *Postmodernist Culture*, 1989, Blackwell, p.8

[2] Connor, *op.cit.*, p.8

[3] For a more complete critique of Lyotard's brief foray into postmodernist writing, see Connor, *op.cit.*, p.29ff.

[4] Some would argue, as in the field of architecture, that postmodernism is a rejection of the metanarrative of liberal modernism and a return to more conservative historical metanarratives. Hence the rejection of formalism and monism in architectural design. See Connor, *op.cit.*, p.65ff.

So, Jacques Derrida[5], one of the fathers of postmodern literary theory, insists that to approach a text without any guard-rails about its meaning robs the text of any integrity and leaves it suspended in a confusion of infinite possibilities[6]. Before him, Charles Peirce[7], talked of the 'Dynamic Object', in other words that which leads to the very existence of the text, not just its meaning. The 'Dynamic Object' is outside a text and determines the limits within which we can interpret a text economically[8]. It is, in Peirce's words, "the Reality which ... contrives to determine the sign to its Representamen[9]" - the reality which manages to make a text mean what it says.

Having wandered for a century in the confusion of liberal modernism, postmodern literary criticism is returning again to an understanding that meaning is guided and even determined by the metanarrative - the very thing that some Christian commentators are saying postmodernism is rejecting.

A text, then, has to be understood in the context not only of the words surrounding it, but also in the context of the presuppositions and ideas that it carries with it. It must be understood in the context of the metanarrative. If we are going to understand what the narratives of the Old and New Testament really mean, we have to understand the metanarrative that is going on *behind the scenes* as it were.

That is not the same activity as suggested by the various historical-critical methods of *Traditionsgeschichte*[10]. These methodologies seek to understand how texts come to be what they are. Using these tools, Biblical

---

[5] See Jacques Derrida, *Of Grammatology*, 1976, John Hopkins University Press, p.158

[6] This confusion is known as "unlimited semiosis" and implies an understanding of texts whereby there is a possibly infinite variety of interpretations. Such semiosis is advocated by the Pragmatist School, especially Richard Rorty. See Rorty, "Ideal and Textualism" in *Consequences of Pragmatism*, 1982, University of Minneapolis Press.

[7] Charles Peirce, *Collected Papers*, 1934-48, Harvard University Press, 4.536

[8] For economic and uneconomic reading of texts, see Umberto Eco, *Interpretation and Overinterpretation*, 1992, CUP.

[9] Representamen means "what a word/sign refers to".

[10] Namely, the methodologies of textual criticism, source criticism, form criticism and redaction criticism.

critics have often focused their attention on a text to determine its authenticity, originality and so on - and so affect the acceptability and authority of a particular text.

However, the study of metanarratives is not the preserve of the source, redaction or form critic. Metanarratives are of use to Biblical critics because they provide the context in which a particular text is to be understood - using a different metaphor, the canvas on which a particular text picture is painted. Understanding metanarrative as the theological, philosophical and sociological context of a text leads to a hierarchy of narrative strata:

Metanarratives	the broad canvas	the overarching context, concept or presupposition
Narratives	the picture	the focused text that is actually read
Sub-narrative	the media used	the ingredients that go into making up the narrative - style, form, comments, characters, plots, rhetorical devices

There is always the fear that as a postmodern idea of metanarratives develops within Biblical studies, we are going to find ourselves pushed further and further into subjectivism. However, the point of Biblical study is to look at the text itself, determine its meaning, examine its structure, deduce its teaching, and, amongst all the apparent dissection, revel in the wonder of it all. Bible critics traditionally deal for the most part with the picture itself spending only a limited time looking at the canvas and the medium used. If we are to begin to look under the picture to the canvas, then this looking will be the duty of each Biblical Critic. It may be that everyone will find a canvas of their own choosing. Like the oft-quoted warning about the Quest for the Historical Jesus - when you look into a well, all you see is a reflection of yourself. A liberal critic may well find a liberal metanarrative to latch onto; an evangelical will find an evangelical one and so on - pure postmodernism in text critical form!

However, the hope for this line of Biblical exegesis is that metanarratives sidestep theological niceties and pigeonholes. For example, if we look at the narrative of the Good Samaritan[11], we will discover a number of metanarratives: interpersonal and social relations, the role of the dispossessed in ancient peasant society, the responsibilities of the wealthy, or even the role of poverty in Israel. None of these would necessarily be the preserve of any particular theological position[12].

Metanarrative provides the basis upon which, or the context within which the authors of the various parts of the Bible structured their thoughts and wrote their books[13]. It is the foundation upon which all narratives and sub-narratives are built and must be understood to further understand the lower classifications. Ultimately, metanarratives have to be determined by a close study of the contexts of the narratives of the Bible - the theological, philosophical and sociological contexts. If one metanarrative is to replace that traditionally accepted by the Church, then it will have to survive such close scrutiny of the text and not simply rely upon the odd proof text here and there.

With this in mind, I will now turn from methodology to practice and attempt to view each of these issues in light of the various metanarratives that underpin the proof texts that people tend to pluck so ruthlessly out of context.

---

[11] Luke 10:25-37

[12] Although I am aware that the emphasis on wealth and poverty reflects my own social reading of Luke's Gospel.

[13] For a consideration, and rejection of presuppositionless authoring of texts, see James Dunn, *The Living Word*, SCM Press, 1987, chapter 1.

Study Guide for Chapter 1

1. Read Genesis 1-2

2. The passage deals with a number of relationships
   God and Creation
   God and Humanity
   Human and human
   Man and woman

3. What are the charactersitics of each relationship?

4. All four are distinct metanarratives - can you trace them roughly through the Bible?
   e.g. God and Creation: Genesis 1, Fall (3), Noah (9)....New heaven and new Earth (Rev 21)

5. Only the final relationship metanarrative mentions sexual activity. What is distinctive about this relationship?

Chapter 2
Divorce

To set the picture, there are evidently some major differences in the Church over what to do about divorce. Often these differences reflect different metanarratives being used. I remember well my preparation for Circuit Ministry in the late eighties. When we talked of the problem of remarriage of divorced people, for I think that that is the area of discussion and not necessarily the subject of divorce itself, it was clearly argued that although the Bible said such and such, these texts should be seen in the light of the Bible's emphasis on starting again, on the efficacy of repentance, on not rejecting anybody. Therefore a distinct metanarrative, or series of metanarratives was applied.

The first two of these metanarratives are, perhaps, unassailable. The Bible is certainly undergirded with an emphasis on starting over again[14] and on the related subject of the efficacy of repentance[15]. The whole *Heilsgeschichte*, the salvation history of Israel, culminates in Jesus, the final promise, the final answer, the only way to break the cycle - and of course his message was, without doubt, the call to a new life, to a fresh start - repent and believe, come and follow me.

However, the third metanarrative offered is not so much the result of an objective reading of the text but rather a reflection of either liberal modernism or of the overfamiliarity characteristic of the more cuddly end of evangelicalism. There is not a metanarrative of 'not rejecting anyone' in the Bible. I phrase it in the negative to avoid dismissing the obviously correct metanarrative of universal acceptance. There is a paradox, one of

---

[14] For example the whole concept of the covenant - apostasy - promise - repentance - covenant cycle in the Old Testament as evidenced in Hosea 11 among other places, as well as the judgement/restoration pattern inherent in Isaiah. See John 3 and Jesus' discussion with Nicodemus about being born from above/over again. See Paul's talk of the old passing away and the need to put on the new person in Ephesians 4:22-24 and Colossians 3:9-10.

[15] For example: 2 Chronicles 7:14, Isaiah 55:7, Ezekiel 18:21, Luke 23:43, Acts 2:38, Acts 3:19.

the central formative paradoxes of Christianity, whereby God offers universal acceptance to all while making it quite clear that there are those who will not be accepted at the end because of their negative or inadequate response to this offer. So, the consequence of a negative response can be seen in the Parable of the Rich Man and Lazarus in Luke 16 for example, and that of an inadequate response can be seen in the Parable of the Sheep and the Goats in Matthew 25, although these examples are simply the tip of a very large iceberg. A metanarrative based on a God who does not reject is a metanarrative which avoids reading the text.

What then are the texts, the narratives, concerning divorce and remarriage? Divorce is mentioned in the following places: Deut. 24:1, Ezr 10:3, Jer 3:1, Mt 5:31, 19:7, Mk 10:1-12, Lk 16:18, 1 Cor 7. The Deuteronomy text sets the scene by making it clear that a man can write a certificate of divorce and send his wife out from his house even if only on the grounds of finding out something indecent about her. In fact, the text is primarily concerned with remarriage - if the woman remarries and her next husband gets rid of her as well, or dies, then she cannot return to her first husband. That is the point of this verse, of this narrative - reflected in both of the other OT references.

When Jesus comes around to this issue, within the corpus of teaching now referred to as the Sermon on the Mount[16], he takes the first part of the Deuteronomy reading concerning the administrative details of how to divorce someone, and reflects upon the subject of divorce in order to emphasise the sanctity of the marriage union - he quotes a sub-narrative in order to turn people's attention to the narrative and then to the metanarrative[17]. He is not happy simply to reflect upon the mechanics of divorce and remarriage, as the Sadducees found out when they asked him a convoluted question about an overly married and most unfortunate young woman[18]. In that context and in this one, he turns to the actual issue that

---

[16] Matthew 5:31ff

[17] The narrative in Deuteronomy 24:1ff. concerns divorce. Jesus quotes part of the narrative - the sub-narrative concerning the certificate of divorce. On Jesus' use of the metanarrative rather than concentration on the sub-narrative, see Andrew Cornes, *Divorce and Remarriage*, Hodder & Stoughton, 1993, p.195f.

[18] Mt 22:23ff

underlies the question - from the sub-narrative (the certificate) to the narrative (on divorce) from the narrative (divorce) to the metanarrative (the sanctity of marriage).

Jesus does exactly the same in the other Gospel reference to divorce in Matthew 19:3-12[19]. There, when quizzed on the law concerning divorce, Jesus makes it clear that the certificate method was granted because of human weakness and that divorce is against God's design. Mark and Luke make this an unqualified repudiation of divorce and therefore of remarriage. It is Matthew's version of the teaching that causes the problem by making the famous Matthean exception - 'except for unfaithfulness' repeated both here and in 5:31. Seemingly, if Matthew records the correct teaching, and there is no textual evidence to say that his original text said anything other than this, then Jesus permitted divorce and remarriage if only on the grounds of unchastity/unfaithfulness.

What is more important is that Jesus again turns the issue from the narrative to the metanarrative. In these texts, he looks towards the whole idea of marriage. He makes the point that if marriage is really the union of two people into one, then that union cannot be dissolved (except by one party creating a conflicting union?)[20]. It is the metanarrative that drives the argument for Jesus, not just the mechanics of what is going on in divorce and remarriage. Jesus wanted to emphasise the status and importance of marriage over and above the necessity of divorce provision. The metanarrative is not governed by the narrative but supplies the rationale to change the perspective from the specific problem of how you divorce, to the wider issue of the sanctity of marriage.

Matthew's exception allows for differing interpretations of divorce provision. However, all the Biblical references to divorce and remarriage

---

[19] Parallels in Mark 10:2-12 and Luke 16:18

[20] Teaching reflected exactly in Paul's argument concerning sexual immorality in 1 Corinthians 7. In that context, Paul closely links sexual intercourse with marriage. In other words, sexual intercourse is not acceptable outside marriage and marriage is not envisaged without sexual intercourse. Indeed, sexual intercourse is the way of telling that people are married. Sexual immorality is the narrative but the sanctity of marriage is the metanarrative.

actually point to the importance of and sanctity of marriage. This is an emphasis found widely within the Church and frequently within evangelical traditions. It is the metanarrative that undergirds different narratives and sub-narratives on divorce/remarriage provision.

Study Guide for Chapter 2

1. Read Mark 10:1-12, Matthew 5:31-32

2. What is the main emphasis of Jesus' teaching here?

3. Matthew includes his exception - how does this fit in with Mark 10?

4. Jesus does not overturn or condemn the certificate of divorce provision in Deuteronomy 24. If there was a concession to human weakness then, how about now?

5. Christianity is all about repenting for our sinful state and allowing God's grace to give us a frsh start. How does this fit in with remarriage after divorce if divorce is wrong?

Chapter 3
The role of women in the Church

As we begin our reading of the role of women in the church, it is perhaps worthwhile starting with the broader metanarrative rather than with the actual narratives and sub-narratives.

The narrative of 1 Timothy 2, for example, can be seen as a sub-narrative, part of a collection of ethical and didactic guidance to a young pastor from his elder[21]. This collection, a narrative in its own right, forms part of a metanarrative which is Paul's ministry. We need to look at this metanarrative to discover Paul's understanding and outworking of gender roles within the church community rather than looking simply at the sub-narratives. Moreover, we need to take an even broader look at gender roles within the New Testament to see whether an alternative emphasis is present there.

In Paul's broader ministry, he emphasises time and again the role of all Christians within the body which is the Church. Not only did he emphasise this role in his teaching but also in his practice. So, in narratives such as Galatians, we find the often quoted verse[22]:

'There is neither Jew nor Greek, neither slave nor free, neither male nor female; for you are all one in Christ Jesus'

Nor is there any teaching at all that charismata are assigned only to men. Indeed, Paul's practice seems to reject such a hypothesis. Paul himself appointed female leaders to the churches - Priscilla is just one example, others are referred to in the various personal greetings listed at the end of many of his letters - for example, Apphia ('sister' in Philemon 2), Euodia and Syntyche (among Paul's co-workers in Philippians 4:2-3), Junia (a female name equivalent to the male Junius, and thus a female apostle in

---

[21] For the purpose of this paper we shall call this elder and, therefore, the letter's author, Paul. This is not the place for a major debate on the authorship of the Pastorals. Whether or not Paul wrote the letter, the received text of the New Testament places the comments given within the context of Paul's wider ministry. That is the correct context in which to study the metanarratives.

[22] Galatians 3:28 (NIV)

Romans 16:7), Mary (a toiler in Romans 16:6), Phoebe ('sister' and 'deacon' in Romans 16:1) and Tryphaena and Tryphosa (toilers in Romans 16:12)[23]. Priscilla and her husband Aquila are seen, not just as names in a list, but actually engaged in a teaching role in Acts 18 when they explain the way of God more adequately to Apollos. Priscilla and Aquila act together, the earliest example, perhaps, of a clergy couple - we are not told that Priscilla made the coffee while Aquila showed Apollos his mistakes. They are both given an equal role in teaching.

In the gospels we have no mention of a female apostle[24]. However, the women are the first to see the resurrection and as such are given a pre-eminence over the apostles whom they have to tell[25]. Moreover, the gospel literature contains the stories of women assuming roles that would have been expected of men in the culture of the day - and Jesus accepts the roles they assume without question[26]. Note the story of Mary and Martha[27] where the scandal in the story is not that Mary is lazy and leaves Martha to do all the work, but rather that Mary assumes the role of a man - it would be the male members of the household who would sit at the feet of a visitor and listen while the women did what Martha did. Jesus does not condemn Mary for assuming this role, in fact he says[28]:

'Mary has chosen what is better and it will not be taken away from her'

Jesus is not saying here that male role models are better than female role models. What he is saying is that Mary has prioritised her life and seen sitting at the feet of Jesus as her number one priority - regardless of the role models expected of her. It is in this respect that she has chosen that which is better. She has followed Jesus rather than subordinate her faith to cultural convention.

---

[23] See E.E. Ellis' article on 'co-workers' in *Dictionary of Paul and his Letters*, 1993, IVP

[24] Though note the female apostle Junia in Romans 16:7

[25] In the gospel resurrection narratives, one of the common themes to all four gospels is that it is the women who are the first witnesses to the resurrection/empty tomb - see Matthew 28:1-8, Mark 16:1-8, Luke 24:1-10, John 20:1-18.

[26] For a discussion of Jesus and Women, see ed. Kathy Keay, *Women to Women*, MARC, 1988, p.20ff; Ben Witherington, *Women in the Ministry of Jesus*, Cambridge University Press, 1984

[27] Luke 10:38-42

[28] Luke 10:42

Mary provides an example that could be paralleled in other passages. However, the point is that there is a valid metanarrative throughout the NT that points to a re-evaluation of culture-driven gender roles within the Church community. In this metanarrative, women are accepted alongside men and both genders are given an equal role to play in the kingdom. Such a metanarrative seems to undergird Jesus' attitude to women and the roles which he was happy for them to fulfil. It also seems to undergird Paul's practical missionary activity.

It is in the teaching of 1 Timothy 2 and 1 Corinthians 14 among others that this metanarrative seems to be distorted. So, in our correctly gender-sensitive times, Paul's teaching about women often seems grossly anachronistic and objectionable[29]. However, the line that Paul draws in one of the major passages, chosen for illustrative reasons, 1 Timothy 2, is quite clear and precise - *he wants* women:
- to dress modestly (1 Tim 2:9)
- to learn in quietness and submission (1 Tim 2:11)
- not to teach (1 Tim 2:12)
- not to have absolute sway over a man (1Tim 2:12)
- to be in quietness (1 Tim 2:12)

Paul justifies his position by referring to his own metanarrative concerning the Fall narrative in Genesis that he peculiarly summarises with a reference to the sanctification (surely he cannot mean salvation!) of women through childbirth. Some, from any theological position, may be unhappy with Paul's interpretation of the Fall narrative and his subsequent metanarrative of Adamic purity! Paul's reading of the metanarrative is open to questioning here, at least.

There are a number of points to be made to clear the cobwebs off this text before comparing this sub-narrative with the metanarratives we have already discovered in both Paul's and Jesus' teaching and ministry. Firstly, Paul does not say that this is a general edict on women. He makes the point that it is his view. Notice how he introduces this section and the oft repeated 'I'[30]:

---

[29] See Oden, *First and Second Timothy and Titus*, John Knox Press, 1989, p.92
[30] From 1 Timothy 2:8ff., *my own translation*

'I also want women to dress modestly...let a woman learn in quietness...I am not inclined towards a woman teaching...nor having absolute authority over a man...but being in quietness.'

Notice what Paul is not saying here. It is not God's law that... It is Paul's inclination for a specific situation. It is Paul who establishes this policy and the repeated use of 'I' seems to say, "I know that others do but I don't"[31]. Notice the proper translation of αυθεντειν ('authentein' - to have absolute authority over) and επιτρεπω ('epitrepo' - I am inclined towards) - words that have been more loosely translated in the past - perhaps to prop up misplaced gender stereotypes.

Certainly, in this text, Paul is still far from where many would like him to be in our understanding of gender roles and a proper sense of equality within the Church. His sub-narrative remains in tension with the broader metanarrative on the role of women in the church. Therefore, some modern literary critics of the Bible would want to see this as a defective text - as a text which has been corrupted by a metanarrative of patriarchal subordination of women. And of course, if this *is* a defective text, then where do we go to find the next one? As with any subjective methodology applied to a text like the Bible, literary criticism, like Marcion, can end up cutting up the text so that the critic formulates a text which suits her own ends and provides no challenge to her own point of view.

For those Christians who see truth in a metanarrative of equality, 1 Timothy 2 and 1 Corinthians 14 among others are difficult texts. That difficulty is lessened by a proper translation of the original Greek, but it should not be excused by lame excuses about Paul having a bad day, or his use of a secretary to write his letters. The text is there and must be dealt with - most notably by reference to the localised contexts that Paul is

---

[31] Notice the same insistence on his personal agenda which comes out in 1 Corinthians 14 where he asserts that his policy is simply that practised in 'all the congregations of the saints'. Is this an attempt by Paul to undermine those churches which refused to accept male-only authority against his teaching? Interestingly most modern commentators would see both the 1 Timothy 2 passages and the 1 Corinthians 14 passage as applying directly to the specific situations in Ephesus and Corinth and not as global edict on women's behaviour - see notes below.

addressing[32]. Certainly, the texts in 1 Corinthians 14 arise from practices in the synagogue which have been carried over into house church worship. For a correct understanding of Paul's ministry with and teaching on women, the localised teaching must be taken along with Paul's own practice which we have seen to be far less discriminatory.

Despite the difficulty of these texts, acceptance of the role of women in leadership within the Church is grounded clearly upon a valid Bible-based metanarrative which deals with the whole narrative rather than simply focusing on the sub-narrative and which deals with the whole of Paul's and Jesus' ministries rather than focusing on a few proof texts.

---

[32] See Fee, *1 and 2 Timothy, Titus*, Hendrickson Publishers, 1988, p.72 about the local implications of 1 Timothy 2 and possible links with the Artemis cult in Ephesus (repeated in Oden, *op. cit.*, p.95).

Study Guide for Chapter 3

1. Read Galatians 3:26-29, Luke 10:38-42, 1 Corinthians 14:33-40

2. If possible read some background material on 1 Corinthians 14. A commentary will tell you all about women in synagogues and the cult of Artemis in Corinth.

3. Does your reading affect your understanding of Paul in 1 Corinthians 14?

4. How can we apply Galatians 3:28 to today's society?

5. This chapter deals with a metanarrative of equality. How is that shown in the story of Mary and Martha?

Chapter 4
Homosexuality/Human Sexuality

We all know the proof texts that are dragged up in order to condemn the practice of same-sex sexual acts: Leviticus 18:22, Romans 1:27, 1 Corinthians 6:9, the fate of Sodom and Gomorra and so on. It is perhaps unnecessary to rehearse these. The point has been made quite clearly in the recent Methodist report on Human Sexuality that the Biblical evidence stands against the normalisation of same-sex sexual acts[33]:

"It is safe to conclude that the burden of biblical evidence is to reject homosexuality...it is agreed that the Bible condemns homosexuality"

Each of the texts listed above clearly states that same-sex sexual acts are to be included among the lists of sexual immorality ('porneia'). However, to see why this is the case, it is better to go straight to the metanarrative in order to be able to interpret the narratives and sub-narratives correctly. For me and, I'm sure, for many evangelicals, it is the metanarrative and not the sub-narratives that drive the debate - the so-called 'proof' texts or 'testimonia' are the sub-narratives which are driven by the metanarrative. It is only in the context of this metanarrative that they can be understood completely.

For the metanarrative we need to go right back to the beginning and the narrative of Creation[34]. Whether or not we accept this as a chronological narrative, it is certainly a major statement of the metanarratives that undergird much of the New and Old Testament narratives. Here we have metanarratives of creation, relationship with God, the inherent goodness of creation, the gift of human life, the relationship between humanity and the rest of creation, interpersonal relationships and the Fall. Frequently, it is from this passage that many of the later metanarratives derive their source. Interestingly, it is to this passage that Paul turns for justification of his inclinations on women in the Church, and Jesus turns for his answers about divorce and marriage.

---

[33] Report of the Commission on Human Sexuality, MPH, 1990, points 117 and 123, pp.21f.
[34] Report of the Commission on Human Sexuality, MPH, 1990, point 95, p.17 makes a similar suggestion

What then is there here for us in our quest for a metanarrative to cover the sub-narratives that people have found elsewhere in the Bible concerning same-sex sexual acts? Gen. 1:27 and 2:24 provide perhaps the most important metanarrative concerning this issue[35]. We are told in Gen 1:27 that when God came to create humanity, he chose to create a male and a female. Therefore, he did not create a male and a male, a female and a female. He chose to create two separate gender identities who were to exist together in relationship in the Garden of Eden. Moreover, Gen 2:24 takes this principle further by universalising it:

'For this reason, a man will leave his father and mother and be united to his wife, and they will become one flesh'

Marriage between a man and a woman thus becomes the normative and exclusive interpersonal, sexual relationship[36] (I make the point about *sexual* relationship because that seems to be the point of 'the two becoming one'). It is this norm which provides a strong metanarrative which guides many of the narratives throughout the rest of the Bible - it is the corrective which causes the tension in narratives such as Judah and Tamar[37], Joseph and Potiphar's wife[38], David and Bathsheba[39], the woman at the well[40] and so on. Adultery is wrong because it contravenes the normative metanarrative of the sanctity of marriage between a man and a woman (whoever does the act of adultery). Divorce, likewise, is wrong except in the case of adultery because it again ignores the sanctity of the marriage relationship. The various sexual codes of Leviticus 18 are aimed partly at protecting a small tribe from intermarriage, partly at avoiding ritual uncleanness, but mostly to reinforce this metanarrative concerning the normative relationship[41] - marriage between a man and a woman. Deviations from this normative sexual relationship are condemned within the Bible.

---

[35] As Paul discovered in using them in 1 Corinthians 6 and 7 to map out the normalisation of sexual practice on Corinth.

[36] 1 Corinthians 7:2

[37] Genesis 38

[38] Genesis 39

[39] 1 Samuel 9-12

[40] John 4

[41] Compare this understanding to the rather feeble comments on the Levitical passages in the Commission's Report, *op. cit.*, point 106, p.19

It is this relationship that seems to have been woven into the very fabric of creation and not just at the whim of some civilisational forces which can now, in a different civilization, be undone - without it human life would not exist, indeed all life would be impossible except for reproductively asexual organisms. For the Biblical authors this relationship between two members of separate gender identities is *the* sexual relationship to be protected and nurtured and all other sexual relationships are deemed to be outside the norm and therefore to be seen as a challenge to and rebellion from marriage.

Paul in 1 Corinthians 6 and 7, makes a clear link between sexual intercourse and marriage[42]. Sexual intercourse is the seal of the marriage union and therefore represents marriage itself. Sexual intercourse before marriage or outside marriage is therefore impossible - for sexual intercourse *institutes* marriage. Moreover, marriage is between a man and a woman. Because sex is so inextricably tied to the marriage relationship, any sexual intercourse that occurs outside of the marriage relationship is thus included by Paul among the sexual immoral acts which lead to exclusion from the Kingdom[43]. Homosexual sexual acts are necessarily included in the 'porneia' lists as they exist outside the marriage relationship. In Paul, then, is the complete synthesis between metanarrative and narrative - the exclusion of homosexual sexual acts from normative sexual activity is determined by the metanarrative underpinning interpersonal sexual relationships, the metanarrative of Genesis 1-2.

Of course, in Paul, celibacy and singleness are seen as having a great deal of merit - sometimes because of a misunderstanding of when Jesus was going to return. Celibacy and singleness are issues which remain outside any metanarrative of interpersonal sexual relationships because by Paul's argument they are fundamentally *asexual* relationships. Neither celibacy nor singleness aim to compromise the normative metanarrative for *sexual* relationships because neither of them is a sexual relationship. Superficially, this may fly in the face of some modern thinking about human beings and sexuality - some would argue that all human relationships are sexual. With this in mind, it is very interesting that Paul makes it clear that celibacy and

---

[42] 1 Corinthians 6:16
[43] 1 Corinthians 6:9

23

singleness are appropriate lifestyles only for those who can cope with their own sexuality in a sexless lifestyle. If you cannot cope, then Paul recommends you do not try it! Paul is not saying that humanity is asexual - he is accepting that sexuality is part and parcel of humanity but that it needs to be celebrated in one of two ways - in a sexual way, namely marriage between a man and a woman, or in a way which precludes sexual acts, namely through celibacy or singleness. Paul would regard our inability to maintain these two possible paths as sin.

With this strong metanarrative at hand, which we have seen is talked of again and again in the teaching of Jesus and in the other narratives in the Bible, it is not very surprising that evangelicals talk so strongly against same-sex sexual acts. At every level, the text denounces non-marital sexual relationships. In the Genesis metanarrative we find that the normative sexual relationship is between a man and a woman. If we look at the Biblical narratives, we find that this metanarrative is affirmed once again. And if we look at the proof texts, the sub-narratives, we find once again an agreement against any sexual relationship outside of marriage which remains exclusively as the sexual relationship between a man and a woman - no other form of marriage is countenanced in the Bible[44].

It may be argued that there are other metanarratives that supersede this one: metanarratives concerning universal acceptability, inclusivity of the kingdom and so on. As I have previously stated, in any subjective study the conclusion drawn by one individual will always have to be ratified by the community[45]. This metanarrative is determined by the text - by a close reading of Genesis 1-2 and the teaching on sexuality throughout the Biblical material. It is grounded not upon tradition or human prejudices but upon Scripture itself. Therefore, I would argue that it is not a subjective choice but actually underlies much of what is talked about in the Bible concerning interpersonal sexual relationships and provides the foundation

---

[44] The polygamous relationships of Solomon and others are harshly criticised by the author of Kings (1 Kings 11:3ff), and the more sensitive Chronicler records only one wife (2 Chronicles 7:11) - Pharaoh's daughter - despite the author of Kings recording that Solomon had 700 with 300 concubines.

[45] Even within Rorty's postmodern unlimited semiosis, a reading of a text is of use only when the reader can find a reading community which will validate their interpretation.

for the Biblical condemnation of same-sex sexual acts.

To stop orthodox Christianity opposing the normalisation of same-sex sexual acts, orthodox Christians would have to throw away their Bibles - so ingrained within the material is a metanarrative against same-sex sexual activity and for a normative sexual relationship in marriage between a man and a woman.

Study Guide for Chapter 4

1. In Chapter 1 we looked at a number of metanarratives about relationships deriving from Genesis 1-2. They were:
   1. God and Creation
   2. God and humanity
   3. Human and human
   4. Man and woman

   We noted that sexual activity was mentioned only in the last.

   Remind yourselves of the distinct features of these four metanarratives.

2. Read 1 Thessalonians 4:3-8

   (verse 4 literally means "each should learn to acquire a spouse in holiness and honour" - although the word "spouse" could also mean "vessel")

3. Here Paul is condemning uncontrolled sexual activity. What are the controls that the Bible suggests are appropriate for our sexual activity?

4. How does this fit in with the metanarrative concerning sexual relationships arising from Genesis 1-2?

5. What are the implications for ignoring this metanarrative according to Paul in 1 Thessalonians?

Chapter 5
Conclusion

We have seen that a metanarrative is the theological, sociological and philosophical context of a text. It is the overriding principle which determines the meaning of a text. Metanarratives have been challenged by some proponents of postmodernism but within postmodern literary criticism they are seen as an intrinsic part of understanding the meaning of texts.

Close study of the text determines a metanarrative as we discover the overriding context of the texts themselves. Therefore, by focusing on the metanarratives behind the Biblical texts referring to the three subjects outlined in the title, we have begun to see a clearer picture of the evangelical position on all three.

Firstly on divorce and remarriage, we have seen that an exception clause in Matthew allows for differing perspectives on divorce provision. However, we have seen that the metanarrative referred to again and again is that of the sanctity of marriage. It is this metanarrative which must be stressed and which is stressed in the Christian Church. This metanarrative provides the context in which we should view divorce and remarriage - just as Jesus referred to this metanarrative when he was questioned about divorce.

Secondly on the role of women in leadership in the Church, we have discovered a metanarrative of equality throughout the teaching and ministry of both Jesus and Paul. We find a metanarrative which questions culturally determined female subordination. In this case, we also found texts which undermined this metanarrative. These texts had to be interpreted properly by a correct translation from the original language and also a clear understanding of the local conditions which the author was addressing.

Thirdly, on the issue of human sexuality, we looked at the Genesis metanarrative in which marriage is seen as the normative and exclusive sexual relationship. We also saw how this metanarrative governed narratives relating to sexual relationships throughout the Biblical material.

It is in the context of this metanarrative that we need to consider the 'proof texts' against same-sex sexual acts. Clearly, according to the Genesis metanarrative, such acts are to be included in the list of proscribed sexual practices.

Bibliography:

Andrew Cornes   *Divorce and Remarriage,*
                                    Hodder & Stoughton, 1973

Steven Connor   *Postmodernist Culture,*
                                    Blackwell Publishers, 1989

Jacques Derrida,   *Of Grammatology,*
                                    John Hopkins University Press, 1976

James Dunn,   *The Living Word,*   SCM Press, 1987

Umberto Eco,   *Interpretation and Overinterpretation,*
                                    Cambridge University Press, 1992

Umberto Eco,   *The Limits of Interpretation,*
                                    Indiana University Press, 1990

Gordon D. Fee   *1 and 2 Timothy, Titus,*
                                    Hendrickson Publishers, 1988

R.T. France   *Women in the Church's Ministry,*
                                    Paternoster Press, 1995

Stanley Grenz   *A Primer on Postmodernism,*
                                    Eerdmans Publishing, 1996

Stanley Grenz   *Women in the Church,*
                                    Inter Varsity Press, 1995

David Harvey   *The Condition of Postmodernity,*
                                    Blackwell Publishers, 1990

ed. Gerald Hawthorne et al.,
                       Dictionary of Paul and his Letters,   IVP, 1993

ed. Kathy Keay   *Women to Women,*   MARC, 1988

McCarthy and Clayton *Let the Reader Understand,*
                                    Bridgepoint Press, 1994

Ed McKnight   *Postmodern Use of the Bible,*   Abingdon 1988

ed. Alvera Mickelsen   *Women, Authority and the Bible,*
                                    Marshall Pickering, 1987

Thomas Oden	*First and Second Timothy and Titus*,
	John Knox Press 1989
Charles Peirce	*Collected Papers*,
	Harvard University Press, 1934-48
Richard Rorty	"Ideal and Textualism" in *Consequences of Pragmatism*,
	University of Minneapolis Press, 1982
Philip H. Towner	*1-2 Timothy & Titus*, Inter Varsity Press, 1994
Ben Witherington III	*Women in the Ministry of Jesus*,
	Cambridge University Press, 1984

Some other titles available from

CLIFF COLLEGE PUBLISHING

THE WAY TO PENTECOST
Samuel Chadwick

Throughout his ministry Samuel Chadwick gave exceptional prominence to the doctrine of the Holy Spirit. This book has the characteristic mark of the author, full and accurate knowledge of the Scriptures, clearness of teaching, depth of insight and practical purpose. It cannot fail to improve the mind, quicken the conscience and kindle an earnest desire to receive the gift of the Spirit in his fullness.

ISBN 1 898362 08 4

THE PATH OF PRAYER
Samuel Chadwick

"I have written out of an honest heart, that has sought above all things to be effectual in the communion and ministry of Prayer, and to which there has come no greater joy than the fellowship of the inner sanctuary. I have written out of the experience of my own prayer life, in the hope that what has helped me may be helpful to others." *Samuel Chadwick*. A Cliff Classic and vital book on prayer. ISBN 1 898362 07 6

OVERHEARING THE GOSPEL
Fred B. Craddock

Fred B. Craddock is the Visiting Professor of Preaching and New Testament at Candler School of Theology, Emory University, Atlanta, USA. He is one of America's most gifted preachers and a remarkable teacher in homiletics. His books on preaching are essential reading for anyone committed to preaching the gospel in such a way that its hearing evokes a response. ISBN 1 898362 06 8

TRAVELLING MAN
Paul Taylor and Howard Mellor

(A tribute to the life and ministry of the Revd. Dr. Arthur Skevington Wood)
Arthur Skevington Wood was a Methodist Minister, evangelist, scholar, author, itinerant preacher and College Principal; a man of many gifts. In these pages readers will find information about Dr Wood's life not generally known, which gives insight into his ministry and reflects something of the greatness of this gentle giant of a man - for spiritual giant he surely was. ISBN 1 898362 05 X

THE ART OF EVANGELISM **William J. Abraham**
Following his best seller, The Logic of Evangelism, this new book takes further Professor Abraham's belief that evangelism should involve taking the whole gospel to the whole person. The book reveals his understanding that evangelism is more than winning people for Christ - it is a process of discipleship, introducing new converts to all the riches of the Christian faith. ISBN 1 898362 00 9

BEING A MISSION CHURCH
Philip A. Clarke

Mission must be ongoing activity in the life of the church, or so this book contends. The local church must move from the idea of having a mission to being a mission. These study notes are designed so that you and your church may engage in mission, using the Book of Acts as a model.   ISBN 1 898362 04 1

REVIVAL, TORONTO and the CHURCH TODAY
William J. Abraham, William R. Davies & G. Howard Mellor

For some time there has been considerable interest in what has been called the Toronto Blessing. Is it a work of God or something more sinister? This booklet gives first hand experience and reflection by Billy Abraham, a connection with the ministry of Wesley by Bill Davies and Howard Mellor offers some guidelines for the church today. It is God who gives blessing and we pray that these articles will offer inspiration and wise reflection whether we experience God's blessing in Toronto or elsewhere.   ISBN 1 898362 13 0

EVANGELISM AND THE LOCAL CHURCH
Philip A. Clarke

The best base from which to reach our neighbourhood with the Gospel of Jesus Christ is the Local Christian community, yet much mission activity in local churches appears to be a short term spasmodic appendage to the normal life of the congregation.   This book offers styles, strategies and models which help congregations and leaders to have mission at the centre of the church's life. It offers pointers towards mobilizing the membership for on-going evangelism through... **The Local Church.**   ISBN 1 898362 14 9

DOCTRINAL CONFESSION and RENEWAL OF THE CHRISTIAN CHURCH

This first tract in the series is from the acclaimed scholar Dr **WILLIAM (Billy) ABRAHAM**. The paper exposes the misuse of the so called Wesleyan Quadrilateral and forms a clarion call for Methodists to re-affirm their heritage in the classical Christian tradition. It is essential reading for all who are interested in the present debates and future direction of the Methodist Church   ISBN 1 898362 12 2

CLASSICAL CHRISTIANITY Richard Clutterbuck, Barrie Cooke & Peter
Stephens   The Methodist Church has cherished its heritage as part of the evangelical movement of the last two centuries. Now some of the core foundations of scripture and tradition are being challenged. This book seeks to bring a contemporary statement of Classical Christianity, written by those who represent the evangelical and sacramental heritage of Methodism.   ISBN 1 898362 15 7